Songs
From
the
Black
Meadow

First published in Great Britain in 2014 by
Exiled Publishing, South Street Arts Centre,
21 South Street, Reading, RG1 4QU
Copyright © Chris Lambert October 2014

A CIP catalogue record for this book is
available from the British Library
ISBN-13: 978-1502305398
ISBN-10: 1502305399

blackmeadowtales.blogspot.com
blackmeadowsongs.blogspot.com
lambertthewriter.blogspot.co.uk
exiledpublications.blogspot.co.uk
soullesscentral.blogspot.com

For Kev Oyston, Chris Sharp, Jim Peters, Emily Jones, Oli Cox, Elena Martin, Grey Malkin, Alison O'Donnell, Stephen Stannard, Alexander Roberts, Elena Charbila, Anthony Washburn, Zachary Corsa, Denny Corsa, Mervyn Williams, Angeline Morrison, Clive Murrell, Keith Seatman, Nigel Wilson, Stephen Henderson, Cathy McAllister, Erin Tingle, Mary Tingle, Freya Wilson, Daisy Screen, Phil Hull, Liz Kirkhope, Amy Rushent and Tim Edwards for bringing the Songs from the Black Meadow to life…

Other Works by Chris Lambert

Published by Exiled

Tales from the Black Meadow

Some Words with a Mummy

Published by Verse

"First Step" in Dead Files IV

Published by CFZ

"Pilot" and "The Catalogue" in Tales of the Damned

Published by Stagescripts

The Simple Process of Alchemy

Ugga – A play about a boy with a paper bag on his head

Ship of Fools

Loving Chopin

Contents

Introduction

As the summer leaves began to turn to brown in the latter quarter of 2008, the musician and composer Kev Oyston was walking through the heather on the North York Moors when he made an exciting discovery.

Mr Oyston was very near RAF Fylingdales, an early warning system that is quite naturally shrouded in secrecy. About two miles from Sleights on the A169 there is a little stopping place on the left very near the main entrance to the MOD site. If the mist isn't too high you can see the great Radar pyramid that has replaced the three strange Radomes that dominated the landscape until the 1990s. It is at this spot that the public bridleway shadows the fence line of the MOD property. Stark warning signs dominate, there are CCTV cameras and a certainty that "trespassers will be prosecuted".

On the fence panel of a gate, Kev Oyston discovered a brass plaque that would change his life forever. The plaque revealed information about Professor Roger Mullins, a "Researcher of Black Meadow and its associated phenomena" who went missing from that area sometime after 1st August 1972.

In Memory of
PROFESSOR ROGER MULLINS
Researcher of Black Meadow and its associated phenomena
Last seen here
1st August 1972
Plaque donated by The Rightwater Archive

The mist hung over the heather and the hum of traffic hid another sound. As Kev listened he could hear something else, something underneath, a distant and chilling scream that seemed to go on and on, stretching and spreading over the land with the oncoming mist.

Over the following months Kev Oyston found himself inspired to dig further. He contacted me at the University of York, encouraging me to tell him more about Professor Mullins. He discovered the original master tapes of a lost Radio 4 documentary that shed more light on the Black Meadow, and he was also able to gain access with the help of Chris Lambert and myself to the unique folklore of the area. Chris Lambert put together a book of that folklore and the two of them released a book and album both entitled "Tales from the Black Meadow" to the unsuspecting public in September 2013.

Black Meadow has been compared to a virus. It gets under your skin. In the year following the publication of "Tales from the Black Meadow" musicians and artists were inspired by these new tales to create music and songs of their own. Chris Lambert discovered a new tale entitled *"A Minstrel Came Out of the Meadow"* that has been published to celebrate the release of this new album. I have been very impressed with the efforts of these two men to keep Roger's work alive and I hope that you enjoy your time in the Black Meadow. Do watch your step though and please stay out of the mist.

Professor Philip Hull
Folklore and Esoteric Studies
The University of York

A Minstrel

Came

Out of the

Meadow

A Black Meadow Tale

Chris Lambert

A Minstrel Came Out of the Meadow

As I was watching one darkening eve

Above the purpling sky

The sound of pipes and singing clear

Caught my listn'ing eye

I bent my gaze toward the field

And look'd both left and right

To sight a rustle, a step, a cough

Within the coming night

The bramble to the left of me

Began to shake and grumble

And blackberries ripe and sweet and plump

Began to slip and tumble

I saw a hand, a hand at first

And then a booted foot

An arm, a shoulder and jacket too

Its colour black as soot

He stepped out from the bramble sharp

And stood there gazing bright

His smiling face and voice so sweet

Lit up the dusking night

He walked to me and danc'd a jig

He took me by the hand

He made me dance and dance I did

Upon the dimming land

I could not help but laugh with him

His face so glad and kind

His singing and his merry tunes

Eas'd my weary mind

From where'd he come? I asked the man

He look'd at me askance

And pointed to the bramble bush

And danc'd a second dance.

"From the meadow I have come,

To sing a tune for thee

To make all dance and join my chant

To make all souls soar free."

17

And so he sang a beauteous tune

That made my spirit soar

And then he sang three wonders still

And still I wanted more

He sang of life, he sang of death

He sang of maiden's fair

He sang of war and joy and peace

And deepest dark despair

I grinn'd and clapp'd my weary hands

Ask'd for another song.

And would he sing another then

And stay so very long?

He shook his head and said that

He had other folk to see

That all his skill and artful noise

Were not just made for me

I groan'd at him in angry tones

And said I'd offer gold

The minstrel was not slave to me

Wouldn't do as he was told

I cried and howl'd, I stamp'd my feet

I said I saw him first

He smil'd and grinn'd and told me soft

I'd only make things worse

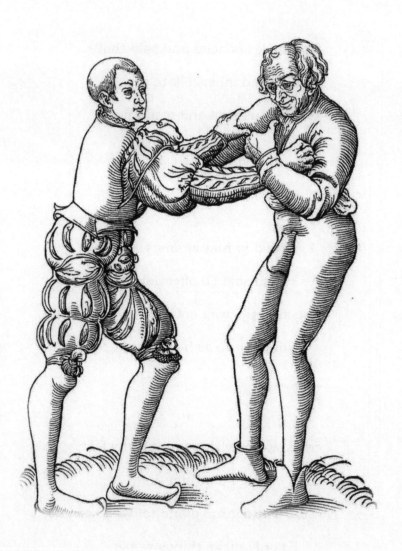

I grabb'd him by the wrist and begg'd him

Sing his songs so good

If he'd not sing for me again

I'd kill him where he stood

He shook his head and played his pipes

And said I'd hear one more

And when I'd heard that final song

I'd want no songs for sure

I'd never want another tune

Nor even want a hymn

And all music that I'd ever hear

I'd desp'rate try to dim

I laugh'd and told him "Sing your song"

And he sang his song so sweet

He sang of love and hate and loss

And vict'ry and defeat

He sang so high, he sang so low

He sang so in between

He sang of life and passion too

He sang of simple dream

He sang with drum, he sang with pipe

He sang with lyre and harp

He sang in minor keys and more

He sang in flat and sharp

He humm'd and roar'd, he cried and laugh'd

He made me weep and when

At last my tears were dry and gone

He sang them out again

He sang out fear, he sang out hope

He sang out all my joy

He sang out all my mem'ries sweet

Of when I were a boy

He sang for hours and ev'ry note

My heart it fill'd and drain'd.

I felt my soul be cleans'd and then

I felt my soul be stain'd.

And now at last the time had come

To play the song's sweet end

He stopp'd and shook his head and said

"I'll leave you now my friend."

I tried to speak, but speaking would

Erase the heav'nly tune

I did not want the echo of

The chords to end so soon

I reach'd for him but he just grinn'd

And skipp'd so fast away

And I slump'd right down upon the ground

And waited for the day

But at dawn the birds all sang

And their song was clear and bright

They threaten'd to erase the song

I'd heard long in the night

The cock it crow'd, it crow'd so loud

The ass began to bray

The lowing cows and bleating sheep

Announc'd the coming day

The church bell rang, an infant cried

A horse began to trot

Its hooves beat out a drumbeat

While the ploughman ploughed his plot

The noise was sour inside my head

A bitter pill to hear

I placed my hands upon my ears

And hummed the tune so dear

But my own attempt it seem'd so foul

Not like the minstrel's art

The tune it floated from my grasp

And broke my aching heart

I ran far from the village loud

Into the meadow's midst

I tried to find a silence there

To find the song I missed

But all those sounds, they tried to take

That blessed song from me

So I ran deep and further in

To let that song be free

And on I ran and on I run

To let the silent mist

Surround my head, engulf my heart

Inside its smoke-filled fist

If I pray for silence will it come?

Will I wait so long?

Allow the tune to fill my mind

And revive the minstrel's song?

...these are
the
fruits
of the
moor...

The Fruits of the Moor

(Winterberry – discovered by Chris Sharp)

V1.
There was a young man who went looking for
work
Bade goodbye to his wife at the door
'I'll bring you' said he 'fine things from the
town'
And with that he set off for the moor.

He'd been walking a while when he sat down
to rest
'Neath the boughs of an ugly old tree
But he jumped with a start as the branches
raised up
And the tree he said 'listen to me' He sang:

C1.
Damsons, blackberries, juniper,
Elderflow'r, gooseberries, sloe.
These are the fruits of moor my friend,
These are the fruits of the moor (these are the
fruits of the moor)

V2.
The man said 'please help, I am heading for
town,
Perhaps you could point me the way?
I'm looking for work so I can buy some fine
things,
Fine things for my wife today'.

'What riches need you with such bounty
around?'
Said the tree with a tone of surprise.
And with that he enchanted the man with his
song
And they married from sunset to sunrise,
chanting:

C2.
Damsons, blackberries, juniper,
Elderflow'r, gooseberries, sloe.
All we need are the fruits of the moor,
Only the fruits of the moor (only the fruits of
the moor)

V3.
Well he lived off the fruits of the moor for a
year,
And a year and a year after that.
The village they thought that his absence was
queer
While his wife she grieved and sat.

Three years to the day, he arrived at her
door,
And now here is the funniest thing:
He opened his hands as she fell to the floor,
And gaily he started to sing. He sang:

C3.
Damsons, blackberries, juniper,
Elderflow'r, gooseberries, sloe,
I've brought you the fruits of the moor my
love,
Brought you the fruits of the moor (brought
you the fruits of the moor)

Outro.
Damsons, blackberries, juniper,
Elderflow'r, gooseberries, sloe.
These are the fruits of moor my friend,
These are the fruits of the moor (these are the
fruits of the moor)

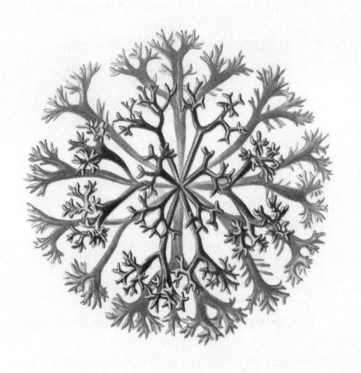

Dark Moss and Coldheart

Emily Jones

Dark moss and coldheart,
Autumn is here.
Under the brambles,
Water runs clear.

And the pale moon's face watches over the
reservoir,
Frosty apple smile.

Black eyes are shining,
Deep in the leaves.
Teeth are for tearing,
Sunlight deceives.

And the cold moon's face watches over the
reservoir,
Icy apple smile...

Dark moss and coldheart,
Shadows crisp and curled,
Softly the evening,
Closes round the world.

Search the Fields

Elena Martin

Search the fields
Go to the fields
Find the girl before the mist finds you.
Search the fields
Walk on the fields
Find the girl, find the missing few.

Oh the fog is rising still
In the air there hangs a chill
If at once the cold wind blows
The village comes the village goes
Over where the brambles lie
Thorns that grow and seem to cry
Oh the brambles tough and wild
Screaming as a new born child

Search the fields
Mist on the fields
Find the few the fog has taken in.
Search the fields
Walk on the fields
But do not follow the mist as it welcomes you in

Oh the fog is rising still
In the air there hangs a chill
The village rises through the haze
Who will know how long it stays

43

Black Meadow Song

Grey Malkin

Where did you go?
Down to the Black Meadow
You are not alone
Down in the Black Meadow
Where no flower or tree does grow
From the Black Meadow
Hear the song of crows
All through the Black Meadow

We'll all go
To the Black Meadow
One day all will go
To the Black Meadow
We reap what we have sowed
In the Black Meadow

Faces in the hedgerow
Down in the Black Meadow
Hear the North wind blow
Down in the Black Meadow
Figures dancing heel to toe
Across the Black Meadow
One day we'll all go
Down to the Black Meadow

We'll all go
To the Black Meadow
One day all will go
To the Black Meadow
We reap what we have sowed
In the Black Meadow

We'll all go
To the Black Meadow
One day all will go
To the Black Meadow
Arm in arm and row on row
To the Black Meadow

Song of the Horseboy

Chris Lambert

Yesterday
You were one of the people
You were one of the people
Who told them to dance

Yesterday
I was drawn to the meadow
I was drawn to the meadow
And started to dance

Yesterday
You were one of the people
You were one of the people
Who cried as I danced

Yesterday
I walked out of the meadow
I walked out of the meadow
And taught you to dance

The Meadow's Call

Stephen Stannard

Travel through the night, waiting for the light
to strike the standing stones, and now we are alone.
Carved spirals to be found, leading you to be bound.
No path to point the way, this is your dying day.
And you can see the hoards breaking through
and their twisted claws grasping you

There's no way to escape the need for you to stay,
as the meadow hunts you down.
A bramble from the bough, plants you 'tween the
ground.
Clawing at the bone, for all that has been done

The cold burns deep inside, reaching from another
time.
Splinters slither in. There is bark instead of skin.
Married to the wood. This yoke is well and good,
to cling to from my arms, this meadow and it's farms.
And you can feel the hoards tether you,
and their twisted claws are now you

There's no way to escape the need for you to stay,
as the meadow hunts you down.
A bramble from the bough, plants you 'tween the
ground.
Clawing at the bone, for all that has been done

I can't close my eyes to all the meadow has to bring.

I am dead inside and I hunger for the spring.

I lost my place in time now the rot is setting in.

I want to see some light and I hope you will begin

to raise me from this hole.

Save me, let me roam.

Wrench me from this hole,

raise me and take me home, home, home, home

Our Fair Land

(Traditional English)   *Arranged by Mervyn Williams*

56

Mist and Heather call us soft
Over bramble meadows
Village field and apple loft
Under land and hedgerows

Will you not hear the call?
Will you with us stand?
Will you take our hands in yours?
Wake our fairest land.

Hidden cave and darkened sphere
Rag and bone and scream
Shining apples hold no fear
For this waking dream

Will you not hear the call?
Will you with us stand?
Will you take our hands in yours?
Wake our fairest land.

Church bell rings out and proud
Horse hooves tramp in sweet time
Voices, drums that play so loud
Trap their dance in sweet rhyme

Will you not hear the call?
Will you with us stand?
Will you take our hands in yours?
Wake our fairest land.

Welcome to the meadow

Oli Cox

VERSE 1
I pull up, headlights are my silhouette,
the demons in my mind telling me I shouldn't get out
yet,
I follow instinct I know that there's a job to do,
the body's on the back seat it will look at you.
I get out and a slam the door behind me,
wearing gloves cover tracks they won't find me
the shovel's grip between my fingertips pull her out
lay her on the ground smell the air as I look around
once the coast's clear that's when I grab her feet.
not a thought in what I'm doing it's become routine
I drag her body with the weapon on my shoulder,
we're only going for a drive is what I told her,

CHORUS
Welcome to the meadow
you won't leave with your mind intact,
Welcome to the meadow
once you arrive there's no turning back,
Welcome to the meadow
close your eyes as they're keeping track,
Welcome to the meadow
Welcome to the black meadow

VERSE 2

The corn becomes my camouflage,
night worker the day is out here to sabotage
my eyes sting cold winds in the air of March
that is when I get the paranoia kick in avalanche
I reach the graves of victims,
really the feeling is so addicting
blood thickening, why do I find it riveting
living it daily I just know you would find it sickening
I start to dig, moonlight on my back,
I really dig, this kind of attack
little did she know that she was picked from a pack
I'm underneath the queen, that's why the press call
me jack
get it? I'm feeling for those who got it,
my mind is calling me normal my soul is labelled
psychotic
someone is watching the police have they found me?
no it's my victims that surround me

CHORUS
Welcome to the meadow
you won't leave with your mind intact,
Welcome to the meadow
once you arrive there's no turning back,
Welcome to the meadow
close your eyes as they're keeping track,
Welcome to the meadow
Welcome to the black meadow

VERSE 3

As they rise from the dirt
their eyes filled with hurt
they get revenge on their killer,
now the role is reversed
As they rise from the dirt
their eyes filled with hurt
they get revenge on their killer,
now the role is reversed

CHORUS

Welcome to the meadow
you won't leave with your mind intact,
Welcome to the meadow
once you arrive there's no turning back,
Welcome to the meadow
close your eyes as they're keeping track,
Welcome to the meadow
Welcome to the black meadow

Launched on October 21st 2014, the new album **Songs from the Black Meadow** celebrates the work of 17 musical artists from around the world. The artists work in a variety of musical genres and are all inspired by the legends and myths of the Black Meadow.

The Black Meadow is a piece of heathland located on the North York Moors, just next to the Early Warning System at RAF Fylingdales. It is a place steeped in folklore and mystery. This is place where many people have gone missing, swallowed up in the dense mist. Black Meadow is renowned for strange phenomena such as a ghostly village, time-slips and bizarre transformations. You could find yourself trapped there surrounded by horsemen, meadow hags, bramble children or creatures made from the fog itself...

Tales from the Black Meadow is a collection of stories and poems gathered about this strange place. In late 2013, Reading author Chris Lambert invited musicians and singers from around the world to contribute to this collection, to celebrate the strange stories from this mysterious region. The artists hale from Ireland, Scotland, Kentucky, North Carolina, Greece, Newcastle, Yorkshire, Cornwall, Devon and Reading. In their exciting musical styles from folk, to instrumental, to drone to rap to choral; they have captured the essence of this dark and forbidding place.

For more information about this release or the Black Meadow Phenomena contact Chris Lambert
Email: blackmeadowtales@outlook.com
Phone: 07722441705
You can also visit: Blackmeadowsongs.blogspot.com

For more information about the Black Meadow visit:
blackmeadowtales.blogspot.com and brightwaterarchive.wordpress.com

"The stand out entries include "Beyond the Moor" a poem about a maiden accosted by a bandit who remains unafraid due to having been to the "beyond" of the title and returned. Also of note are "Children of the Black Meadow" where a bereaved mother resurrects her deceased kids as blackberry bramble homunculi; cyclical damnation tale "The Coal Man and the Creature" and the paranoia-inducing sucker punch "The Watcher From the Village" ... this is a collection that strongly invites a second reading.." - STARBURST MAGAZINE

"A banquet of weirdness..." – Hypnobobs

"...visceral dread slowly rises from its mustiness..." – Mythogeography

"A fine piece of British Hauntology" - Gareth Rees Author of Marshland

"Properly spooky and really well written." - Sebastian Baczkiewicz - Creator of Radio 4's Pilgrim

"Tales from the Black Meadow" features a blend of weird and disturbing short stories. This collection is well worth checking out for its originality and chilling tone." - Phil Syphe Author of Cash 'n' Carrots and other capers

"...very atmospheric black and white illustrations courtesy of Mr Nigel Wilson" – Hypnobobs

"Lambert manages to create genuine atmosphere and spine-tingling moments... but he also injects some black humour and much appreciated wit." Steevan Glover - Author of The Frog and the Scorpion

When Professor R. Mullins of the University of York went missing in 1972 on the site of the area known as Black Meadow atop of the North Yorkshire Moors, he left behind him an extensive body of work that provided a great insight into the folklore of this mysterious place.

Writer Chris Lambert has been rooting through Mullins' files for over ten years and now presents this collection of weird and macabre tales.

Marvel at tales such as The Rag and Bone Man, The Meadow Hag, The Fog House, The Land Spheres and The Children of the Black Meadow.

What is the mystery surrounding The Coalman and the Creature?

Who or what is The Watcher in the Village?

What is the significance of the Shining Apples?

Why is it dangerous to watch the Horsemen dance?

Beautifully illustrated by Nigel Wilson these tales will haunt you for a long time to come.

"Can you tell me, maiden fair Can you tell me if or where I shall see my child again Walk upon the fields of men? Will she ever stumble back From the meadow all a'black?"

"Tales From the Black Meadow takes this idea one step further, providing an actual CD of music to accompany the stories. All but one track is named after one of the tales and the music of each complements its narrative counterpart. The slight scratchy crackle of the music effectively dates it, making it sound as though it could have been copied from a vinyl record from the '70s. ... atmospheric precision..."

Andrew Marshall - Starburst Magazine

"Listen to Tales From The Black Meadow and be introduced to the strange and wonderful world of Hammer Horror, of British Folklore, of Radiophonic Scores and things that go bump in the night. A delirious and delicious mystery..."
Forest Punk

"An irresistibly evocative title that no budding hauntologist could rightly ignore.."
The Active Listener

"To me, it easily sounds like the opening to a television show from the late 70's. I can see the title card and the credits appearing over gently revolving images...One could still listen to the record and have a sense of the supernatural and the uncanny; dark foggy nights can be heard in the muted tracks. Little details give the songs on Tales from the Black Meadow their spooky spice, such as the soft crackling on each track, giving it the feel of an old vinyl record..."
Fascination with Fear

"Tales From The Black Meadow is one of the best releases we had this year, with ten marvellous compositions to state it.."
Music Blob (Blog)

"If you enjoy a bit of Folklore, Poetry, A Mystery on the moors, 1970s kids TV and some very lovely haunting music, then this book and CD are an absolute must.."
Keith Seatman - Test Transmission

When Professor R. Mullins of the University of York went missing in 1972 on the site of the area known as Black Meadow atop the North Yorkshire Moors, he left behind an extensive body of work that provided a great insight into the folklore of this mysterious place.

Mullins, a classics professor, had a great interest in Black Meadow, in particular its folklore and spent many years documenting its history and tales that were part of the local oral tradition. In his office, his colleagues found over twenty thick notebooks crammed with stories and interviews from the villages around Black Meadow.

Some of these stories seemed to be from the legendary disappearing village itself and provided some vital clues as to how the phenomena was interpreted and explained by the local populace.

In 1978, Radio 4 produced a now rare documentary about the folklore, mystery and tales surrounding the Black Meadow area. It also featured music specially commissioned to accompany the programme. This music has recently been unearthed by the Mullins Estate and carefully isolated for your listening pleasure.

These stories, poems and songs have also been gathered together to capture the unsettling nature of the Black Meadow.

Do not listen to this on your own at night and make sure you shut your windows. Listen for the stamping feet of the horsemen, avoid the gaze of the Watcher in the village and do not walk into the mist.

14385722R00042

Printed in Great Britain
by Amazon.co.uk, Ltd.,
Marston Gate.